Columbia Scholastic Press Association

Box 11, Central Mail Room Columbia University New York, NY 10027-6969

Magazine Fundamentals 3rd Edition

Edited by
John W. Cutsinger, Jr.
and

Official CSPA Scorebook
for Student Magazines

Poynter Institute for Media Studies
Library
JAN 27 '94

Name of Magazine _____

School or College _____

Street Address _____

City _____ State _____ Zip _____

Type of School

☐ College or University

☐ Senior High School

☐ Junior High School

☐ Other (specify) _____

Summary

	Maximum Score	Your Score
Concept	(150)	_____
Content	(500)	_____
Design	(300)	_____
Creativity	(50)	_____
Total	(1000)	_____

All-Columbian Awards ☐

Rating _____

An Introduction

The first publication in the magazine field to be issued by the Columbia Scholastic Press Association appeared in 1943 under the title **Primer of School Magazine Technique**. It was prepared by John J. Snowcroft, then-Director of Journalism at Central High School in Paterson, New Jersey. The second venture, **Magazine Fundamentals**, edited by Eve B. Bunnell, also of Central High School, was published in 1952. This second edition was reprinted with minor corrections in subsequent years and with some more significant changes in text and scoring in 1973.

The objective of both the **Primer** and the 1952 and 1973 editions of **Magazine Fundamentals** were the same: to outline the basic principles involved in writing, publishing and management of a successful student magazine. Additional explanation is given for how this type of publication is judged.

For this third edition of **Magazine Fundamentals** the Association has sought the assistance of an outstanding young teacher, John W. Cutsinger, Jr. of Westlake High School, Austin, Texas. During a decade of teaching experience in three Southwestern states, Cutsinger has earned top state, regional and national honors for successful advising of student newspapers, yearbooks and magazines. He brings to this edition of **Magazine Fundamentals** a generous enthusiasm tempered by considerable experience.

His manuscript received careful reading by two dozen outstanding advisers and members of the Association's Board of Judges. Their suggestions were coordinated by Edmund J. Sullivan, director of the Association. Prof. J. F. Paschal of the University of Oklahoma served as a primary reader and deserves special recognition. Particular appreciation is extended to Helen Smith, adviser to **Mirettes**, Newton North High School, Newtonville, Massachusetts and to Joyce Woodfield, adviser to **Impressions**, Parkville High School, Baltimore, Maryland. Additional appreciation is due to Josephine Yingling, Bel Air, Maryland and to Dr. Russell Jandoli, Professor of Journalism at St. Bonaventure University, St. Bonaventure, New York. A vote of thanks is also due to those advisers who have volunteered their time and talent as judges to assist in evaluating the annual magazine entries in the Association's contest/critique.

Edmund J. Sullivan
Director of the Association

Magazine Fundamentals and Official CSPA Scorebook for Student Magazines by John W. Cutsinger, Jr.
Book design by Deanne C. Bauer.

Copyright © 1984 by: Columbia Scholastic Press Association
Box 11, Central Mail Room
Columbia University
New York, NY 10027-6969.

All rights reserved. No part of this book may be reproduced in any form—except for brief quotation (not to exceed 1,000 words) in a review or professional work—without permission in writing from the publisher.

ISBN 0-916084-15-9

Manufactured in the United States of America

Third Edition

First Printing: September 1984

Magazine Fundamentals

Part one: Concept

Magazines have taken on more sizes and shapes throughout their history than any other student publication. They began as general reports of school news and activities; later, they became showcases for student literary and artistic talent. In recent years, the total design and concept of magazines has dramatically changed, and both the overall concept and format have been modified. Student staffs now have a wider range of perspectives from which to approach this type of publication.

Certain basic concepts apply to each type of magazine. The goal of all efforts is to produce a publication that appeals to its audience and follows sound principles of writing, editing and design. Whether it be a literary-art, a general interest or a specialized magazine, the content and presentation must be carefully planned and executed by the staff.

In their study of professional magazines, Click and Baird offer an example of an overall editorial concept and how that concept then defines the magazine's formula.

A plan to serve women with information and features that will help them at home, in self-improvement, and in their careers provides a basic concept for a magazine. From this editorial concept evolves a formula developed from a plan and policy decision about the kinds of content the magazine will carry, the readers it will cater to, and the kinds of advertisers it will attempt to attract.

Before the staff can plunge into these areas, they must organize themselves into a directed, purposeful group. To be organized, a staff must define their goals or editorial concept.

Defining Goals

The staff must define their goals in a realistic manner. What is the basic editorial concept for this magazine? The entire staff might help to compile a written statement of goals.

What does the staff hope to accomplish with the magazine? Who are the readers for this magazine? Answering these two questions will suggest a specific format to use. Different magazine formats serve the needs and wants of different readers.

Literary magazines publish strictly literary works such as short stories, poetry and essays. Literary-art magazines include these genres while adding art in various media, such as pen and ink illustration and photography.

Special interest magazines offer a mixture of prose, poetry, essays, interviews and feature stories. Foreign language magazines offer part or all of their content in one or more foreign languages as a means to showcase student talent and achievement in languages other than English.

Departmental magazines publish nonfiction examples of student work in academic subjects such as history, sciences or mathematics. Folk magazines follow the model developed by Elliot Wigginton in the **Foxfire** series, offering intensive coverage of local artisans, craftspeople and senior citizens in an effort to highlight and preserve community traditions.

Each of these different formats is created by a different set of goals. Different goals lead to different policies and operating styles.

DRAMATIC DESIGN combines a dominant photograph, primary and secondary headlines and an identifying caption for portraits to create a stunning introduction to a feature story. (**Athens Magazine,** Ohio University, Athens, OH 45701)

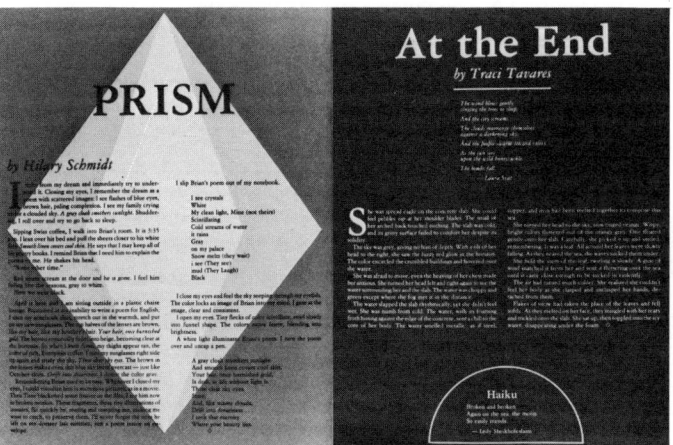

SIMPLE GEOMETRIC SHAPES used with screens (left) demonstrate how the least contrived designs are often the best. ALL TYPE REVERSED against screened background (right) offers another basic choice using only black ink and white paper. (**Heritage,** James Madison High School, Vienna, VA 22180)

Concept—3

Policy Statements

The policy statements should govern all aspects of magazine production. To write the policy statements, the staff must answer certain key questions.

1. What are the format requirements?
2. What are the editorial assumptions?
3. Who and what should be accepted? Should it include only work from creative writing classes or only voluntary submissions or a mixture of both? Should it include work by alumni or community members? The limits should be clearly stated and followed by the staff.
4. What are the staff's responsibilities as writers and journalists? Professional standards should be adapted to the level of ability possible in the school or college.
5. What are the procedures for selecting materials to include in the magazine?
6. Who will make the selections? Editors? Editors and staff? Editors, staff and adviser(s)?

Once the staff has defined its general goals (or editorial concept) and written specific policy statements (the editorial plan), it must select a format and create production specifications.

Establishing Format

What is the format? Format considerations include the physical dimensions of the magazine, number of issues per semester or year, number of pages per issue, paper stock for both text and cover, the color of inks and methods of typesetting and binding.

When determining format, the staff must carefully consider each choice it makes. How cost-effective will each choice be? Printing is a custom process with each printed "job" priced according to its particular requirements. Hasty decisions or inattentiveness to the specifics of the format will be costly later on, both in terms of money and the time required for the printing process itself. Early in this process, the staff should submit bid specifications to several printers. They should then list sources of income. Based on this budget, the editors will decide on the best printing method and the quantity and page size of issues per year.

Format specifications should be firmly established and recorded in the bid before it is submitted to prospective printers. The more professional the specifications, the more accurate responses the staff can expect. It may be possible to cut costs substantially if the staff sets the type and reproduces the art using its own facilities.

While there are hundreds of important choices that must be made, many of which involve finances, there are some absolutes that apply to all magazines.

The Adviser's Role

While some schools and colleges have the luxury of a structured program for the sole purpose of producing a magazine, volunteers staff other student magazines as an extra-curricular activity.

An adviser must assume only the role indicated by that title. This means offering one's expertise and providing a healthy atmosphere in which the staff will work to the best of its ability. Simply put, the adviser does not edit the magazine nor does he or she work as a staff member.

Some magazines have more than one adviser. In these cases, advising duties are often split between editorial and business advisers or between literary and art advisers. These positions can work effectively as a team if the separate positions are carefully defined and if responsibilities are shared by colleagues who respect one another.

Since the adviser often assumes the role without prior experience, it is crucial that the adviser be enthusiastic about the publication. If the adviser treats the magazine as a "stepchild" and fails to give it the necessary attention, the staff may follow suit.

In cases where the publication does not have an adviser, the student editor should seek the counsel of a faculty member, a professional writer, poet, designer or photographer or experienced student editors of other campus publications. While such a person (or persons) will not function as an adviser in a formal sense, it is often helpful to have someone who can answer questions or provide a second opinion in moments of uncertainty. The magazine can only benefit from this additional input.

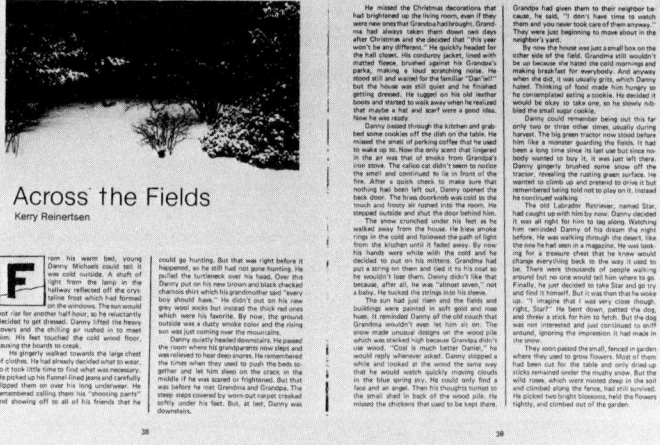

BALANCED DESIGN offers the basics for any spread heavily covered with text. A mood photograph is placed to attract the reader's eye to the beginning of the story; title and author's name mark a design transition from photograph to the initial letter "F" which opens the text.

The Editor's Role

Editing a magazine is no easy task. There is no ideal pattern for the organization and management of a staff nor is it a simple process to select, edit, design and reproduce material. From issue to issue, these needs change as should the composition and structure of the staff.

The adviser should discuss job descriptions with potential editors. By so doing, the adviser can reduce the problem of peer pressure that often occurs when a staff does not recognize that an editor is taking his or her job seriously and responsibly. Advisers should explain to those interested in the various editorial positions the importance of the responsibilities and tasks associated with these jobs. A potential editor should recognize that the position will entail both planning and hard work.

For example, job descriptions might say:

Editor-in-chief: in charge of the publication. Oversees the management and production of the magazine.
Literary editor: oversees the solicitation and subsequent details of handling the literary submissions.
Visuals editor: oversees the solicitation and subsequent details of art and photography.
Design editor: conceives and executes the design concept of the magazine.
Business manager: coordinates all business aspects of the magazine including advertising, circulation, sales and finances.

Other positions may be created by dividing assignments of the above such as a production editor, a subscription or circulation manager, a copy editor. All of these responsibilities must be clearly defined. The generalizations above are incomplete because each staff will fashion its own organization, depending on its needs.

The Role of the Staff

To help the staff operate smoothly, a list of responsibilities should be published and distributed to prospective members. These job descriptions must

4—Magazine Fundamentals

provide enough detail to enumerate major duties the staff must complete so that it works successfully as a team. Such a common understanding eliminates the later excuse that someone did not know what was expected of him or her.

One method for determining the suitability of a staff member for an editorial position is to assign simple tasks for the applicant which will be evaluated by the adviser and/or experienced staff members.

Organization of the staff depends on those who volunteer or who can be drafted for the staff. Once commitments have been made, the staff can begin to take shape. The adviser should facilitate, but not dictate, this process.

Title Page

Every magazine should have a title page that draws a relationship between the cover and the inside, providing the reader with essential information concerning the publication and, like the cover, helping to set the tone. The title page should reflect the visual personality of the magazine. Some staffs coordinate the inside cover with the title page to constitute a double-page spread and include the contents listing, staff listing and a colophon.

Basic title page information includes the publication's name which is usually the dominant type element on the page. Also included are the date, the name of the school, the complete school address including city, state and zip code. The volume number (avoiding Roman numerals) also should appear on this page. So should the frequency of publication, if known.

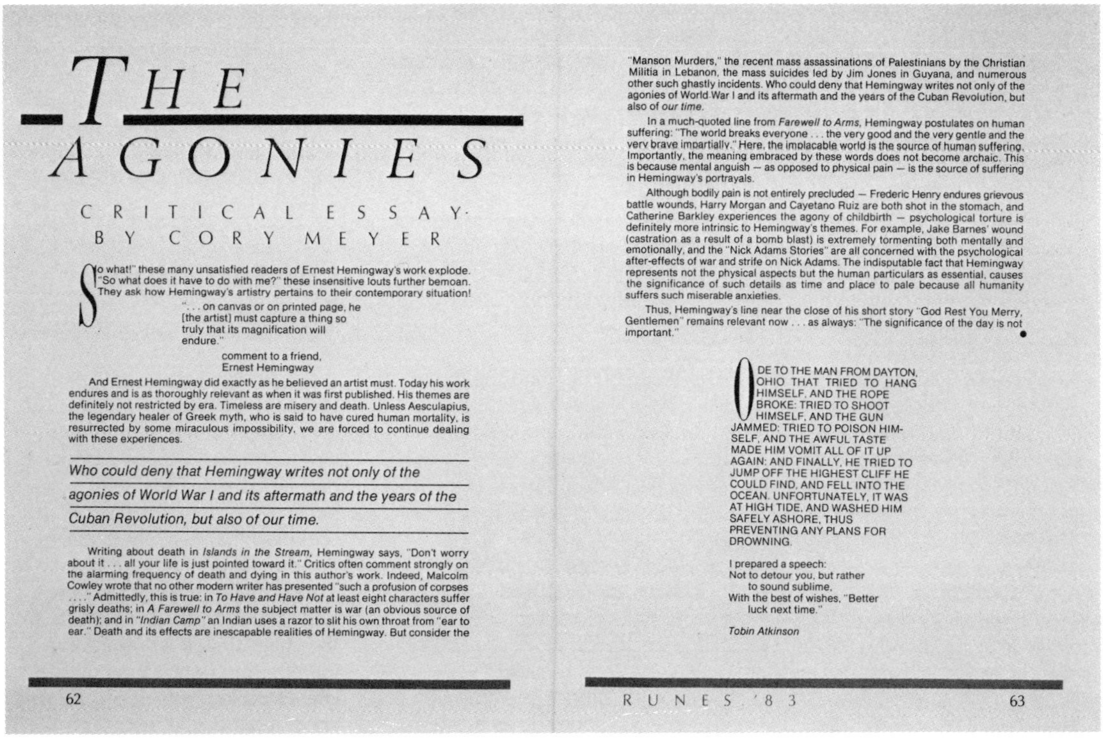

The colophon, if incorporated into the title page, should list publishing specifications that might prove of interest to the reader. This area can also contain press association awards won and the price of the issue. Policies which govern the magazine also can be included.

A WRY TITLE and an obviously improvised photograph entice the reader to pursue a one-page story. (**Athens Magazine,** Ohio University, Athens, OH 45701)

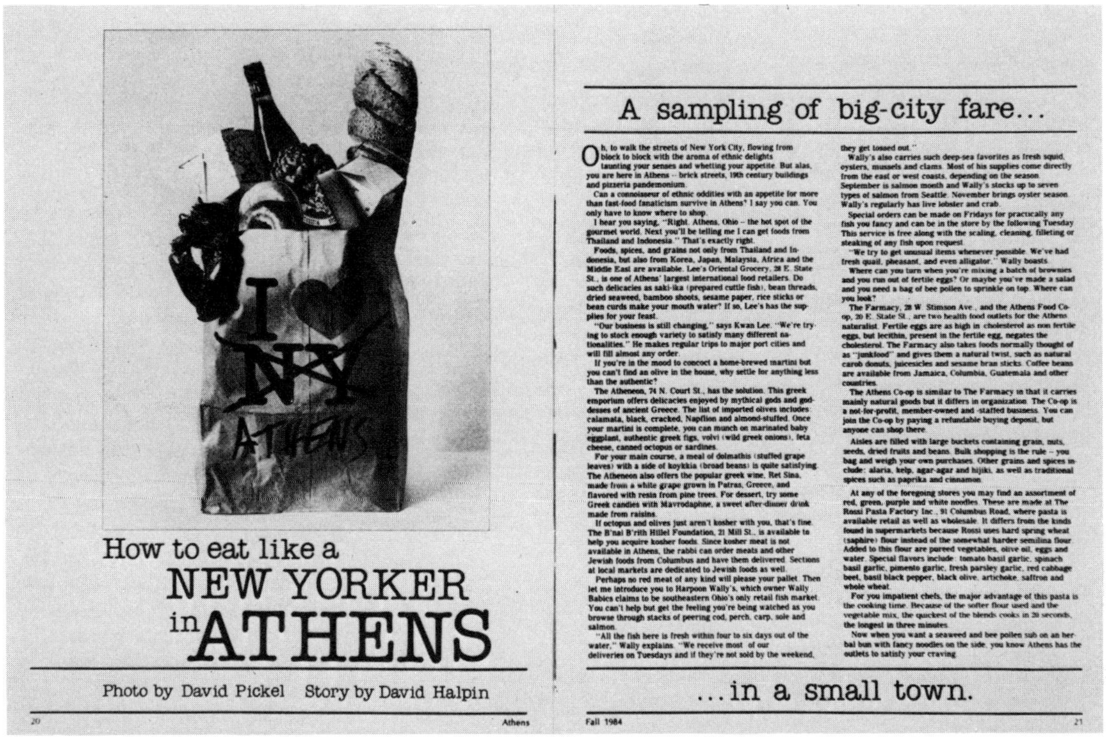

ELEGANT USE OF TYPOGRAPHY unites this spread and sets a tone for reading an essay. The three-line "blurb" uses simple rules and surrounding white space to attract the reader's attention. Large initial letter combines with restrained use of all-caps to separate the poem from the essay. (**Runes,** Brighton High School, Salt Lake City, UT 84121)

Concept—5

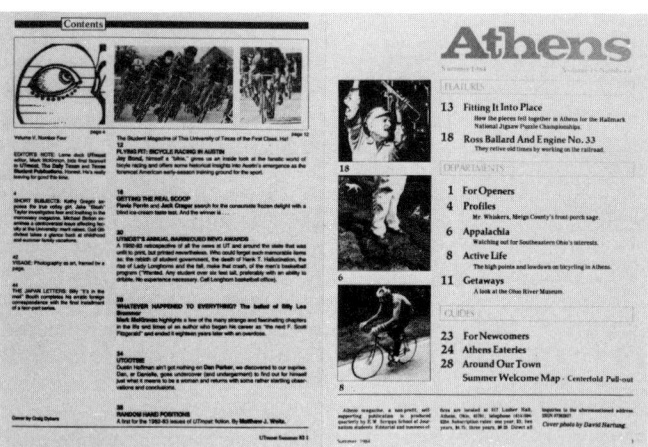

LIVELY GRAPHICS at left lets this contents page sparkle. Notice that volume and issue number, cover credit, folio/folio tab and bylines for all articles provide essential information. (**UTmost,** University of Texas, Texas Student Publications, Austin, TX 78712) VERTICAL ORIENTATION contrasts UTmost contents page at left. Folios under photos correspond to articles listed in contents. Subscription and other vital information is neatly listed at bottom. (**Athens Magazine,** Ohio University, Athens, OH 45701)

FACULTY CONTRIBUTOR is clearly identified by this magazine with separate credit for illustrator placed logically. Simple rule lines achieve spread linkage. Story offers a first-person approach to the other point of view of a student trip. (**Sunstone,** Spring Valley High School, Sparkleberry Lane, Columbia, SC 29206)

STRONG DOMINANT VISUAL provides a focal point for the reader's eye. This feature magazine uses a thick-and-thin rule to frame the top of the spread and hairline rules to complete the box. Short paragraphs help speed reading of narrow width columns. (**Manila Folder,** Van Buren High School, Van Buren, AR 72901)

Table of Contents

To make the table of contents inviting, many staffs have adapted catalogue inclusions by form with regard to literary works and by media when dealing with artistic selections. It is best to keep them in numerical sequence within each sub-division. All materials of any type or genre included in the magazine should be listed in the table of contents. Titles should be included as well as the names of authors and artists and page number where the pieces begin.

Design of the contents should blend with design of the magazine. A study of professional magazines can give staff designers insight into the unlimited possibilities for creating an attractive and functional table of contents. Photos and art can be included. So can blurbs that give insight into the pieces. Remember that the contents listing must be a functional readers' service.

Special pages devoted to staff work are no longer acceptable magazine content. To replace such pages, yet give the staff their deserved credit, the staff listing can be incorporated elsewhere in the magazine, often on the contents page(s). Readers should see the staff by their positions and acknowledgements the staff wants to make.

Organizational Touches

Pagination is extremely important to the reader. Note the emphasis contemporary publications place on page numbers and folio tabs. These elements serve readers, adding elegance and personality to the publication's design.

Credit lines should serve as the attribution for every work in the magazine. It is important to identify the author, artist or photographer. All such credits should be typeset in the same manner to achieve unity. Some staffs choose to use one style of credit line for prose, one for poetry and another for art or photography. Credit lines should be a part of the design and should serve their function without drawing attention to themselves and away from the content. Avoid overburning or reversing credit lines over art or photos. With art, the printed line is often easier to read than the artist's signature on the work. Credit lines for poetry generally are set at the bottom of the selection flush right with the longest line of the poem.

From application of the basic principles through the polish and refinement of details, designers must recognize the importance of presentation and forethought.

First Impression: The Cover

The cover of the magazine should catch the reader's attention and keep it. First impressions of any magazine come from that first glimpse of the cover. The visual elements should excite curiosity and stimulate interest in the contents. Avoid disappointing your reader with visually boring interior designs. A dramatic and appealing cover should be followed by dramatic, appealing spread designs.

With that first glance, readers should recognize the publication. The most prominent type on the cover must be the magazine's title. Other essential information such as the volume and number of the edition, the year and a hint of a theme if one exists, should be in smaller type.

The cover is the ideal place to begin the theme or unifying concept of the magazine, if it is to have one. Not all magazines will choose the thematic approach. Some magazines may use this method of selecting and presenting content in one issue, but not in succeeding issues during a given publishing year. Using a theme is only one of many ways to approach magazine content and design. If used, however, it is imperative that it be introduced on the cover and carried forward in internal design. That unifying element should be presented simply on the cover through artwork and words.

Staffs must consider the reader when deciding on a cove

6—Magazine Fundamentals

OUTSIDE COVERS showcase artistic talent, setting the tone for quality of visual content throughout the magazine. (**Heritage,** James Madison High School, Vienna, VA 22180)

COVER PACKAGING offers a wide variety of choices. LEFT, student illustrators depict mathematics as a journey throughout unknown territory. (**Math Bulletin,** Bronx High School of Science, Bronx, NY 10468) **BRIEF CASE** offers a convenient carrying "place" for literary arts magazine. (**Hot Lead,** Ole Main High School, North Little Rock, AR 72114)

design. Many times, a staff will design covers that appeal to them with little regard for readers. Weigh carefully all segments of the readership and think through the goals of the magazine when planning the cover.

Keep the cover simple. If art or photography is incorporated, the staff must choose only that illustration which makes a statement about the magazine. The art or photograph should contribute dramatic impact to the cover and should show the relationship between the outside and the inside of the magazine. The art or photo should be of clearly superior quality—probably the best selection that appears in the entire issue.

If type alone is used, it should be attractive, giving the magazine an interesting personality. Avoid handlettering unless it relates directly and clearly to a theme and the reader will immediately understand that relationship. If necessary, show a rough sketch of the proposed cover to a variety of potential readers prior to its final design. Get some opinions and reactions and incorporate them in the final design.

It is important that the design flows freely from spread to spread and that the magazine be kept visually "alive." Careful use of white space is an aid to balance when it is planned for the outside corners of each spread. Remember that white space serves as an "attention-getter" for a selection if that white space strategically draws the reader to the selection.

ART OR GRAPHICS can dominate the cover. Checkerboard background highlights primitive-style bird depiction on Embryo's cover at left. Simple rules and type offer a contrasting approach on Runes' cover, right. (**Embryo,** The Westminster Schools, Atlanta, GA 30327; **Runes,** Brighton High School, Salt Lake City, UT 84121)

Part two: Content

Soliciting Materials

Staff members must accept responsibility for a direct relationship with their readers. Their goal must be to seek out quality instead of quantity of material.

When the staff is selecting literary and visual work, they should seek out every potential resource for contributions. They should seek cooperation from those associated with academic classes in which writing is stressed. The English department is an obvious possibility, but so are others.

Staffs should use their imaginations. Maybe the science, mathematics or technical vocational departments should be solicited for contributions. Perhaps the foreign language or music department has contributions to make. Any courses that afford students the opportunity to express themselves through original work are potential sources for the magazine. Such work can provide fascinating visuals as well as worthwhile, original writing.

If classes are not a viable source, editors should seek members from student writing, photography or design clubs or writers, photographers, artists and designers on other campus publications as possible contributors.

Various Approaches

It is important to provide for voluntary submissions. While students will profess their material not good enough and would not personally submit an entry to the magazine office, they might use a submission box. Periodic contests might also encourage creative writers to contribute to the magazine and also promote a variety of content.

Magazine staff members should be keenly aware of the need for variety and should be systematic about making the most of their school's potential. If the magazine has an elitist image, the staff should brainstorm about ways to make the magazine represent all kinds of talent in the student community.

A general interest magazine, for example, could use a beat system. Staff members can be assigned the responsibility for incorporating this systematic approach to coverage. First, staff members must determine potential areas that need to be covered. Once this list is established, assignments should be made. A system of recording and filing information for reference should be established. With such a functional system, the staff will know if they are covering their defined territories.

Literary-art magazines need to look for variety in poetry, fiction, illustration and photography. A magazine which used only haiku for its poetry might be quite boring. Dozens of stark pen-and-ink illustrations (with little shading) might strike readers as visually monotonous. It may be harder to locate qualified poets, fiction writers, illustrators and photographers than to organize a news-style "beat" system for a general magazine, but the editors must seek out variety in literary-art forms.

The evaluation of submissions is difficult. In the planning stages it is important that the audience of the magazine be specifically defined. Most staffs assume that the entire body is the audience to whom they must appeal. But is that always true? The staff might perform a formal survey to establish a real picture of its readership. Faculty, administrators, parents and community members are often highly interested readers.

If the magazine is to be sold, be honest and realistic. If the readership is not poetry-oriented, the literary-art magazine format should not be "poetry-heavy." If the audience is not artistically-oriented, then the magazine should avoid an over-emphasis on art. ... Some poetry and some art should be used because readers deserve exposure to all forms of expression. The staff can plan a magazine that is well-rounded and represents the best writing and art students can produce.

Content Selection

Literary works include both poetry and prose. When incorporating poetry, it is important that material has a direct relationship to the interests of the readers and provides them with variety.

Prose offers the reader a variety of styles: short stories, plays, informative essays, first-person accounts or anecdotes, human interest features, personality sketches, surveys, interviews, points of view, editorials and critical reviews and news of the school and community.

Art offerings can include oils, acrylics, pencil sketches, pen and ink, charcoal, etchings and photographs.

When the staff has established a policy for selection, they should follow it and make it known to the whole school. The staff should work to develop a policy that is fair and that sets quality standards from which the staff will operate.

To eliminate decisions being made by a sole staff member, some publications use an editorial board. This group can include staff members and individuals from outside the staff to provide a broad spectrum of experience and perspective. Non-staff members can be selected from many areas of the school. Certainly, students from the art and English departments should be included.

Staffs selecting material can code it to allow for anonymous judging. Anonymity relieves the selection board of the temptation to choose a piece because they know the author or artist. The editor or adviser should take charge of the coding process to ensure accuracy and consistency. Pieces can be assigned consecutive numbers in order of receipt.

The Editorial Process

The staff must define the process by which each literary and visual contribution will be considered. Some staffs incorporate the use of oral readings of materials and set minimum standards prior to consideration of the material. Each entry is then judged by this set of minimum standards. If a piece passes this initial screening, it may be judged a second time with higher standards. The staff should be careful to view each entry on its own merit. General considerations should also include the following:

1. Reader Appeal
   Is the topic interesting to the publication's audience?
   Is the level of the material appropriate?
2. Originality
   Is the material absent of plagiarism or mimicry that is not satire?
   Are the ideas fresh, not derivative?
3. Strong Technique
   Is the writer able to maintain a cohesive structure that includes control of time and place?
   Does the plot evolve in a meaningful way?
   Are characters distinct and tangible?
   Is there a sensitive use of language?
4. Depth
   Is the reader left with the feeling that more is being said than appears on the surface?

The above questions generally can be addressed toward fiction, poetry and essay, with obvious exceptions, such as the omission of plot when discussing an essay. All good writing depends on the fine use of language and the application of a structure: the tree on which a writer hangs his ideas.

Good writing is also recognizable by the sense of depth it expresses. For every line of text there is often a line of subtext; ideas in a piece of effective writing give rise to other ideas. Take as an image the dropping of a pebble into a pond. The point where it falls in is the poem, story or essay. The ripples that emit from the point are endless. This is one of the ways we describe great writing to students in their literature classes.

Continued on page 17

CSPA Critique

Both a Judge's Workbook and Your Scorebook

Because judges use this book for scoring the magazine, erasures and revisions of figures are understandable. In case of obvious mathematical or mechanical errors, ratings will be corrected. Only when released by CSPA is a rating official. The decision of the Board of Judges is final.

Part One: Concept (150 points)

Goals and Policies

1. Is there a basic editorial plan evident throughout the magazine?   20 _____
2. Does the content (both verbal and visual) and the design of the magazine work in harmony with one another to make a unified and coherent publication?   20 _____
3. Did the staff clearly relate the content and design to a specific readership?   15 _____

The Cover

4. Does the cover include the name of magazine and year or volume number?   10 _____

Title Page/Staff and Contributor Listings

5. Does the title page contain all required information including the year of publication, name of college or school, address, city, state, zip code, volume and issue number?   10 _____
6. Does the contents listing include article titles, credits and page numbers?   10 _____
7. Is there a complete staff listing?   10 _____

Reader Services

8. Have pages been numbered in a functional way which serves the reader?   10 _____
9. Has the writer/artist/photographer of each selection been properly credited adjacent to the selection?   10 _____
10. Is it evident that the staff has established a policy and a style sheet to govern the production of the magazine?   15 _____

Judge's Comments and Suggestions for Improvement:

11. Has the staff taken care to avoid trite
    material and plagiarism?   20 _____

Part One Total Points: 150 maximum   (150) _____

All Columbian Award

Judge's Comments and Suggestions for Improvement:

Part Two: Content   (500 points)

The content of any magazine includes both verbal and visual elements. Verbal elements include all prose and poetry; visual elements include art and photography. For the purposes of this evaluation, these two areas will be considered separately.

I. Verbal Content

Magazines offer a great variety of forms of verbal content. Most student magazines fall into three categories: literary, literary-art and feature (or general interest) magazines.

Plan A. Literary magazines offer traditional forms of fiction (short stories) and poetry with an occasional essay. The full allocation of 500 points for Content is therefore evaluated solely for Verbal Content.

Plan B. Literary-art publications add the visual components of art and photography to the literary magazine's verbal content. Half of the allocation of 500 points for Content is therefore given to Verbal Content; the remainder, to Visual Content.

Plans C and D. Finally, feature (general interest) magazines present nonfiction narratives including interviews, essays, columns and editorials. They may or may not include literary magazine content such as poetry or fiction. Accordingly, their scoring plan offers two alternatives: **Plan C** (with literary selections) and **Plan D** (without literary selections). Each of these plans offers a total of 350 points for Verbal Content.

A. Fiction and Narrative

(Literary magazines (Plan A): 225 points; Literary-Art magazines (Plan B): 100 points; Feature magazines with literary material (Plan C): 40 points) Circle plan used.

                                         A   B   C   D

1. Does the action focus
   upon believable char-
   acters through which
   the reader can experi-
   ence the story?   50   30   10   XX   _____

10—Magazine Fundamentals

		A	B	C	D	
2.	Has the plot been carefully developed showing control of time and place, sense of coherent structure and dramatic tension?	50	20	5	XX	_____
3.	Does the language used contribute to the tone of each piece?	30	10	5	XX	_____
4.	Does the language used contribute to clear expression of the content or does it distract the reader by calling attention to itself?	20	10	5	XX	_____
5.	Is the language used overly derivative of major known authors or has it gone beyond simple imitation?	20	10	5	XX	_____
6.	Is there evidence of originality and fresh ideas?	30	10	5	XX	_____
7.	Is there evidence of concise editing to strengthen writing style?	25	10	5	XX	_____

B. Poetry

(Literary magazines (Plan A): 225 points; Literary-Art magazines (Plan B): 100 points; Feature magazines with literary material (Plan C): 40 points)

		A	B	C	D	
1.	Is there a variety of subject matter as focus for the poetry?	50	20	10	XX	_____
2.	Does the poetry show sensitive word choice that results in strongly visual language?	45	15	10	XX	_____
3.	Are literary techniques such as metaphor, simile, etc. used successfully?	45	30	5	XX	_____

Judge's Comments and Suggestions for Improvement:

		A	B	C	D	
4.	Is there a variety of form and approach?	30	15	5	XX	_____
5.	Is poetry fresh in concept, not derivative?	30	10	5	XX	_____
6.	Has poetry been edited to eliminate "dead wood"?	25	10	5	XX	_____

C. Essay

(Literary magazines (Plan A): 50 points; Literary-Art magazines (Plan B): 50 points; Feature magazines with literary material (Plan C): 20 points)

		A	B	C	D	
1.	Is an appealing literary style inherent in essays?	15	15	6	XX	_____
2.	Is there purpose and direction in the content?	10	10	5	XX	_____
3.	Are the essays structured to introduce and develop an argument through use of supporting details?	10	10	3	XX	_____
4.	Are the author's arguments summarized?	10	10	3	XX	_____
5.	Are good transitional elements used?	5	5	3	XX	_____

D. Feature Sections

(Feature magazines with literary material (Plan C): 250 points; Feature magazines without literary material (Plan D): 350 points)

		A	B	C	D	
1.	Has the staff obviously defined the purpose and direction of content?	XX	XX	30	40	_____
2.	Is material designed to appeal to a target audience?	XX	XX	30	40	_____
3.	Does it use sufficient detail and example to hold that audience?	XX	XX	30	40	_____

Judge's Comments and Suggestions for Improvement:

Second Printing with corrections, 1985

12—Magazine Fundamentals

	A	B	C	D

4. Is all material based on authoritative and sufficient research? XX XX 25 40 _____

5. Does feature material provide content which adds depth and variety to the magazine? XX XX 25 40 _____

6. Do headlines attract readers with strong verbs and nouns while avoiding mere labeling of articles? XX XX 15 20 _____

7. Do leads present the most important angles of stories, avoid unimportant facts, and are they varied in grammatical structure? XX XX 15 20 _____

8. Are direct quotations incorporated and are they adequately attributed? XX XX 15 20 _____

9. Are editorials or commentary based on fact and do they present solutions? XX XX 15 20 _____

10. Are interview-related articles interesting, clear in purpose and do they capture the character of the person or event? XX XX 15 20 _____

11. Are reviews well-researched and has the writer demonstrated the expertise to express an opinion? XX XX 15 20 _____

12. Is all material approached from a fresh, creative angle? XX XX 20 30 _____

Judge's Comments and Suggestions for Improvement:

II. Visual Content

(Literary-Art magazines (Plan B): 250 points; Feature magazines (Plan C and D): 150 points).

Art

	A	B	C	D

1. Does art/illustration serve an editorial purpose? XX 40 25 20 _____

Critique—13

	A	B	C	D

2. Is art/illustration the result of strong visual technique and does it have impact?   XX 40 20 20 _____

3. Does art/illustration show evidence of adherence to composition requirements (dominance, balance, flow)?   XX 30 10 10 _____

4. Are visual themes in artwork fresh and not imitative or trite?   XX 40 10 10 _____

Photography

All Photographs

	A	B	C	D

5. **Contrast.** Do all photographs have proper contrast, exhibiting a wide range of tones (from white to black) and avoiding an overall gray or muddy look?   XX 20 10 10 _____

6. **Clean.** Are all photographs free from specks, scratches, spots and fingerprints?   XX 20 10 10 _____

Creative/Mood Photographs

7. Does the degree of focus and/or depth of field in the photograph aid its desired effect?   XX 20 5 5 _____

Illustrative/Feature

8. Do feature photos center on action-oriented content?   XX XX 15 15 _____

9. Does every feature photo have a caption which completes the story that has been started by the content of the photo and clearly identifies all persons?   XX XX 10 15 _____

Judge's Comments and Suggestions for Improvement:

14—Magazine Fundamentals

	A	B	C	D	
10. Are all photographs in sharp focus, exhibiting proper depth of field?	XX	XX	10	15	_____

Overall Effectiveness of Art, Illustration and Photography

	A	B	C	D	
11. Does each piece demonstrate effective handling of the medium and exploration of the technique's limits?	XX	15	10	10	_____
12. Is there a variety of techniques used, given the publication's budget?	XX	10	10	5	_____
13. Are both representational and abstract artwork presented?	XX	5	XX	XX	_____
14. Are art, illustration and photography the result of strong visual technique and do they have impact?	XX	5	5	5	_____
15. Does each piece demonstrate good composition?	XX	5	XX	XX	_____

Part Two Total Points:
500 Maximum   (500)   _____

All Columbian Award   ☐

Part Three: Design   (300 Points)
All Plans

1. Is the quality and weight of the paper stocks (for cover and inside pages) appropriate for the type and illustrations used? 10 _____
2. Does the magazine have an overall visual appeal? 20 _____
3. Have the basic elements of design (dominance and visual organization) been important in the planning of the cover? 10 _____
4. Is the name of the magazine easily read on the cover? 10 _____
5. Does the title page present design elements which link the cover with the inside of the magazine? 10 _____

Judge's Comments and Suggestions for Improvement:

Critique—15

6. Have facing pages been visually linked into single spreads? 20 _____

7. Do external margins create a planned look? 20 _____

8. Has inner spacing been established and consistently used to promote cohesion of elements? 20 _____

9. Does each spread incorporate a dominant element which attracts readers and keeps their attention? 35 _____

10. Is the typography for spreads consistent (unified by family fonts or design similarities)? 20 _____

11. Is a minimum of 9 pica-width/maximum of 23 pica-width observed? 20 _____

12. Do titles/headlines serve as attention getters for the content? 5 _____

13. Are they designed attractively? 5 _____

14. Is there consistency in title/headline typeface? 5 _____

15. Is there consistency in headline style (up or down)? 5 _____

16. Does the use of white space appear to be planned, and is it used effectively? 35 _____

17. Have contemporary graphic techniques been used in a functional and attractive way? 50 _____

Part Three Total Points: 300 Maximum (300) _____

All Columbian Award

Judge's Comments and Suggestions for Improvement:

Part Four: Creativity (50 Points)
All Plans

The CSPA judge will award points here for the staff's ability to produce a magazine whose whole effect is greater than the sum of its parts, especially in relation to experience, time and budget limitations as made known by the self-analysis portion of the membership application and entry form submitted by the magazine.

50 _____

Part Four Total Points: 50 Maximum (50) _____

All Columbian Award

Continued from page 8

The Editorial Problem

The policy for submission and acceptance of material should include the right of the staff to edit material once it is approved for inclusion in the magazine. Some staffs ask contributors to sign an agreement to this effect. If used, this agreement should include a statement which verifies the originality of the submission and confirms that plagiarism has not taken place.

For written submissions, editing may include rewriting to meet the publication's style specifications and correction of errors in grammar, spelling, punctuation and sentence structure to improve clarity. No editing should occur that alters the meaning of the literary piece.

There is a difference between "revision" and "editing." A revision should be the rewrite or rework of the piece by the originator based on suggestions made by the staff. Editing should be any changes which the staff undertakes to make.

All visual contributions, such as art and photography, are also subject to revision. Cropping, proportioning and placement of visual work should be at the discretion of the staff and the contributor should clearly understand that policy.

Organizing the Selections

Before the staff can begin the process of picturing the selections as members of the unit called the "magazine," they must decide how to impose order on the parts. This process appears simpler than it really is. Editors should consider certain questions. The answers to these questions are crucial to the editorial excellence of the finished magazine.

1. In what sequence will we put the pieces?
2. What contributions make sense as groups?
3. With what do we want to "open" and to "close"?

Some selections naturally group themselves—they

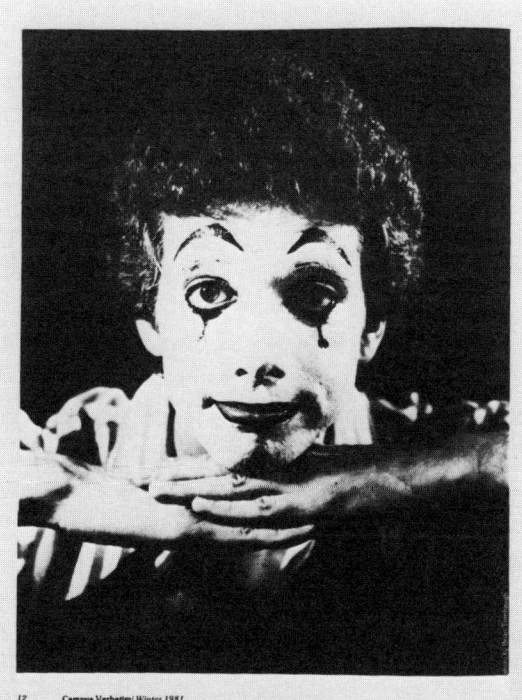

DOMINANT PHOTOGRAPH and clever headline design and placement combine to give this story an eye-catching appeal. (**Campus Verbatim,** Ball State University, Muncie, IN 47306)

FEATURE COVERAGE by a college general interest magazine uses primary and secondary headlines with two photographs: one dominant, the other, small but strategically cropped and placed to introduce the story. (**Athens Magazine,** Ohio University, Athens, OH 45701)

Content—17

LOCAL HISTORY offers a slice of "cultural journalism" in this Oklahoma high school magazine. Design uses simple rules, captions for each photo and large initial letter to begin headline. Smallest photo breaks module around copy. (**Sandscript**, Charles Page High School, Sand Springs, OK 74063)

ELEGANT DESIGN joins a short story and photograph although their content is unrelated. Note the use of serif and sans serif type in the title, byline, initial letters, body type and caption type. (**Runes**, Brighton High School, Salt Lake City, UT 84121)

CONSERVATIVE USE OF COLUMNAR DESIGN uses a news-style approach to planning the spread. (**Athens Magazine**, Ohio University, Athens, OH 45701)

18—Magazine Fundamentals

"belong" together. All staffs are grateful for such "naturals." The problem is that of finding the "transitions," pieces which help carry the reader from one group of "naturals" to the next.

One method of bridging is to look for pieces which have transitional elements such as similarities of tone, mood, theme, setting or plot situations which will captivate readers as they shift their attention from one selection to another.

Another method is grouping pieces by theme concepts: Love, Death, Fear, Loss. The staff must then decide in what order to present these themes. One drawback to this organizational plan can be ten selections on a subject such as Death, for example. If much submitted material is pessimistic in outlook, the staff should give careful thought to maintaining variety within the groups before settling upon this particular organizational plan.

Other grouping techniques will suggest themselves to the staff. All should be discussed and weighed until the organization to be used is decided upon by staff consensus. Balance and harmony of selections must be carefully weighed when arranging the magazine's contents.

Part three: Design

Designing the Magazine

Even the best material will not get the attention it deserves unless the editors present it in the most functional, visually-exciting manner possible. The challenge of the magazine designer is to provide the best presentation for each selection and at the same time create consistency and a personality for the publication.

The staff's first production task is one of **revisualization.** They must cease to think of the individual elements (e.g., illustration, prose, poetry, ads, etc.) that make up the content of the magazine. They must, instead, begin to see the surfaces upon which those elements will be grouped as a whole—like a landscape which contains trees, bushes, clouds, birds, grasses—which on first viewing is visualized as a whole, an entity. Later, a more leisurely inspection of its parts will reveal the unique characteristics of each piece.

In considering how to design the magazine, the staff must first view the magazine through the reader's eyes. The unit first viewed by the reader will be the pairs of facing pages looked at when glancing through the magazine. These pairs of facing pages are called "double page spreads" or DPS, for short. If they fail to form attractive, appealing visual units, the reader will not linger to sample the parts of each DPS, just as a traveller does not pause to inspect a panorama that holds nothing to arrest his or her attention.

If the visual impact of the spread is chaotic, with undisciplined pieces all clamoring for attention, the reader may feel that it would take too much effort, too much concentration to make the plunge into that competitive jungle—he won't know where to start, so he'll solve his problem by ignoring it.

If it is too empty, too arid, he may form the impression that nothing of value was planted here and move on to a more verdant field. The staff should try to make each page a "memorable landscape"—one which holds the reader's attention and gently pulls him or her into the individual elements which are segments of the double page composition.

The designer should have direction and purpose. All design techniques should serve the purpose of enhancing content, instead of "decorating" it or interfering with it.

The Double-Page Spread

Plan all facing pages in the magazine as single visual units. Here the designer should incorporate one or more of three basic techniques:

1. Run a photo or art across the gutter area. Staffs must be careful that the printer can "register" the pages so that the bleed

across the gutter does not leave awkward spacing between the two pages nor that the fold cuts into an important area of the illustration or photograph.
2. Establish a horizontal line which runs across the width of a double page spread. This should fall in the top or bottom half of the spread, but never at the halfway mark.
3. Achieve unity through the use of graphics. For example, include a rule line or use a screened background to link facing pages, or run the title or headline across the gutter.

Every spread in the magazine should incorporate the vital elements of design. They are based upon the eye-flow pattern natural to Western culture—left to right, top to bottom. Designers can better assure visual success by carefully combining type, white space, photos and art on each spread. Every selection should be titled or headlined. A title may simply label the selection with a noun. A headline will have both a noun and a verb.

The Dominant Element

On each spread, one of the basic elements should serve as a focal point for the reader. Most often, the dominant element will be either art or a photograph, but when content dictates, type can become the reader's focal point; for example, a dramatically graphic title or headline. The dominant element serves as a point of reference from which the reader considers all other material on the spread.

Dominance must be planned and executed with caution, taking care that the chosen element is dominant in size and content as well as placement on the double-page spread.

Columnar Planning

Readers have become accustomed to columnar designs in professional magazines. To give your readers that same planned look, consider columnar format. Above all, content should dictate incorporating the columnar format for maximum readability. The reader is uncomfortable with lines of type, especially single-spaced, which are longer than three and one-half inches. Once a specific column width has been established for a particular selection, it should be followed consistently. Columns can and should change depending upon the selection. Generally, nine picas (1½ inches) should be the minimum column width for copy with 21 picas (3½ inches) as a maximum width for standard nine or 10 point copy.

Columns will give any magazine the look of a planned package. Staffs should take care not to visually bore the reader by using only one column design throughout the entire magazine. Designers should be flexible with the use of several column widths varied throughout the issue.

To establish unity, the staff should maintain consistent margins. In the outside margins, leave adequate space at the bottom to accommodate the page numbers or folio tabs. Side and top margins should be consistent from spread to spread. Bleeds should extend to the edge of the page's trim line. Inner spacing between elements serves as a unifying device throughout the magazine and on each individual spread. Either a one or one and one-half pica spacing (but not both) should be kept between all elements on a spread.

The Functions of Typography

Designers recognize the importance of type as a basic element of design. To choose an attractive, easy-to-read type is the designer's prime consideration. Consistency is the keyword. Body and headline type should add to the overall unity of the magazine.

Type should be considered on three levels: body (or text) type, display or headline type and emphasis type (such as art or

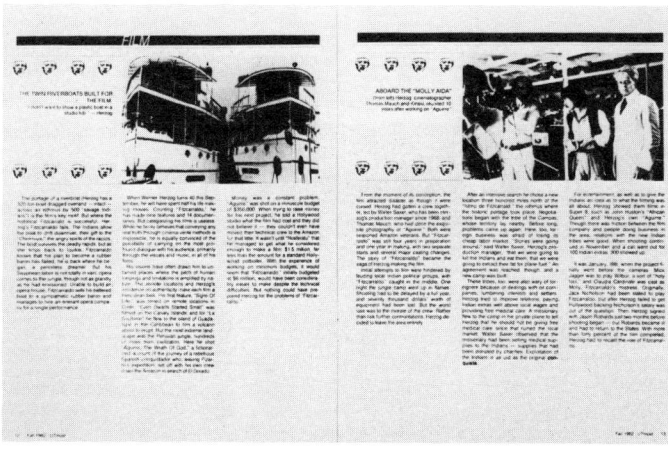

SYMMETRICAL DESIGN can achieve a pleasing unity and harmony if used sparingly. Here random depth columns of copy are topped by a broad horizontal eyeline: 2-column photographs with ragged left, right justified captions. (**UTmost,** University of Texas at Austin, Austin, TX 78712)

LESS IS MORE: a single story occupies this spread, making generous use of white space to set off a single photograph which crosses the gutter, thereby unifying the spread. Simple rules and several initial letters lead the reader into the story. (**Reveille,** Eastwood High School, 2430 McRae Boulevard, El Paso, TX 79925)

VIVID USE OF PHOTOGRAPHY AND TYPE begin a personality profile. (**Athens Magazine,** Ohio University, Athens, OH 45701)

Design—19

COLUMNAR DESIGN WITH A DIFFERENCE varies the width of columns to accommodate horizontal and vertical photographs. (**UTmost,** University of Texas at Austin, Austin, TX 78712)

UNUSUAL PHOTO CONTENT gives designers a focal point for the spread. Here three-quarters of the spread is occupied by a photo of a remarkable habitat: a reconstruction of a Celtic hut. Title and copy identify and amplify the dominant visual content. (**Athens,** Ohio University, Athens, OH 45701)

decorative). Body type ranges from 8 point to 12 point and is used with prose and poetry body copy. Generally, display or headline type ranges from 14 to 72 points. Emphasis type can give the magazine its own personality. Such type can be used for the title, standing headings and page numbers or folio tabs. Titles or headlines for poetry should all use the same size and style of type. Place a premium on the design of titles or headlines offering the reader a visual variety.

In general, avoid handlettering in a magazine. While it may add a personal touch, it often takes on an amateurish look and detracts from the selection. There are occasions when handlettering (especially well done calligraphy) can be used but be certain that the content dictates its use.

Staffs can solve the problem of designing poetry by thinking of the poem as a solid rectangle of type with the end of the longest line serving as the place to put the right margin. By envisioning the poem as a solid rectangle, its placement becomes much easier. When designing spreads of poetry, avoid "butting" titles (placed directly side-by-side) and coordinate poetry with illustrations. Poems should be placed on the spread so that the titles do not fight for the reader's attention. Place them so that white space goes to the outside of the pages. The reader must be able to identify art or photography which serves as an illustration for a poem by its strategic placement.

For longer prose selections, avoid massive columns of lengthy copy, unrelieved by any graphic devices, illustrations or photographs. Use initial letters frequently (but not with each paragraph).

Designers might wish to put a final touch to each of the longer selections with the use of an endmark. A tiny symbol which reflects the personality of the magazine, the endmark serves as a symbol to the reader that the selection concludes. Not all styles of design require an endmark. It is simply one of many typographical devices available to the student designer.

20—Magazine Fundamentals

The Effective Use of Graphics

Graphic techniques serve a wide variety of purposes, but each must function to enhance rather than eclipse the presentation of the material. Graphics are a means for communication, not an end in themselves. Properly used, they can be a powerful tool for the designer to guide the reader through the magazine. Poorly used, they can confuse, annoy and ultimately so frustrate the reader that he or she will give up the attempt to decipher the selection, or even the entire magazine.

Some graphic techniques include rules of varying thicknesses (usually from hairline to 3 points), initial letters, boxes (rules top, bottom and both sides of text or photo), screens (varying percentages of the inks used on the spread), and spot color. Reverses (usually white type on solid ink background) or overburns (darker ink on lighter background) should only be used when readable.

The cost of graphic techniques should be carefully discussed with the printer prior to their use. Techniques such as reverses, overburns, screens and spot color can be quite expensive, especially when their use is not carefully planned in advance of printing and binding.

Part four: Creativity

Since creativity is a quality demonstrated in the areas of concept, design and content, it must be considered when scoring those areas. A display of creative thinking is also evident in the magazine's overall personality. In the creation of a personality for the magazine, the staff shows its ability to foster meaningful connections in the reader's mind, to be imaginative, and to concretely express that imagination.

ACTION PHOTOGRAPHY pulls the reader's eye in the desired direction: from left to right across the spread. Italic type in headline also moves the eye from left to right. (**UTmost,** University of Texas at Austin, Austin, TX 78712)

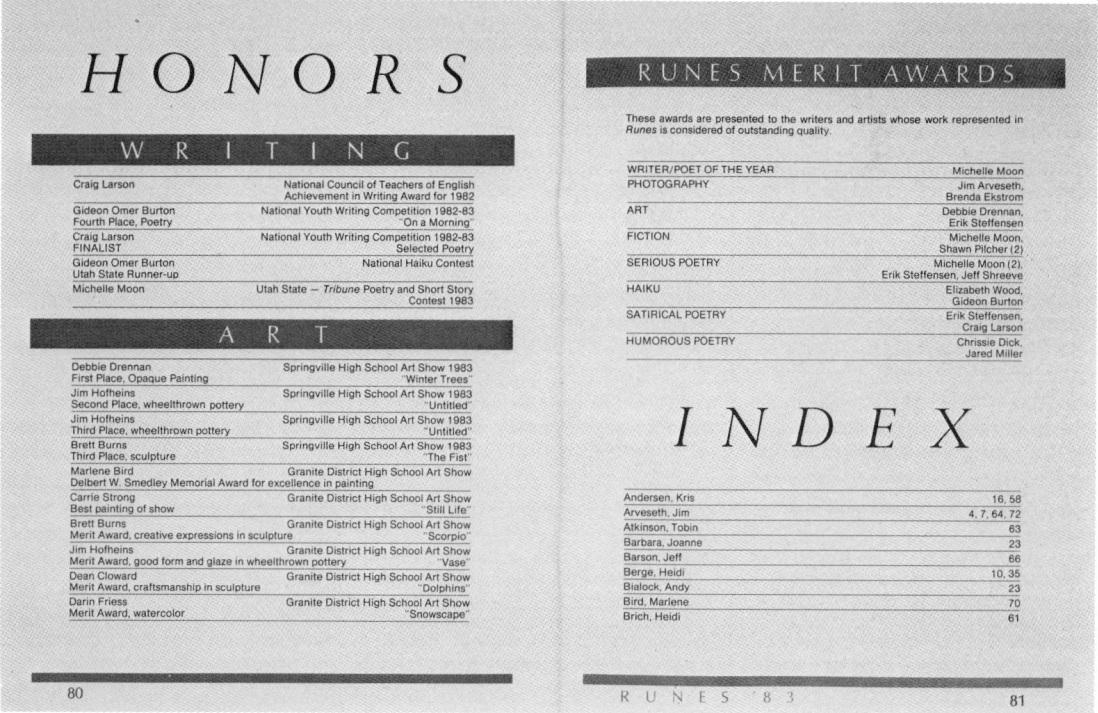

DISTINCTIVE CONTENTS/INDEX SPREAD lists awards and distinctions of contributors with staff-initiated merit awards and the start of full index of contributors. (**Runes,** Brighton High School, Salt Lake City, UT 84121)

Creativity—21

Glossary

Terms used in writing, editing, design, photography, art/illustration and printing production are sometimes baffling in their variety and complexity. The word "composition," for example, has one meaning for a photographer and quite a different meaning for a typesetter. This Glossary offers a selection of terms which should explain many of the basics involved in design, photography and printing production. For further details, consult the *Dictionary of Graphic Arts Terms* by Patricia Barnes Mintz referred to in the Bibliography.

absorption in paper, the property which causes it to take up liquids or vapors in contact with it. In optics, the partial suppression of light through a transparent or translucent material.

accordion fold in binding, a term used for two or more parallel folds which open like an accordion.

additive color a way of producing most desired colors by different combinations of the three primary additive colors: red, green and blue. See *subtractive color*.

all caps words or type printed entirely in capital letters.

aperture the opening in a photographic lens that admits light and can be varied in size.

art board durable, protective paperbase board on which artwork is mounted or drawn to prevent damage in shipping or handling.

art type commercially prepared acetate-base typographical characters that can be transferred to an art board by cutting or rubbing and submitted for printing as artwork.

artwork any hand-produced, illustrative or decorative material submitted for printing, i.e., drawings, paintings, collages, ornamental typography or borders.

ascender the upper strokes of those lower case letters that extend above the x-height, for example, b, d, h.

author's alterations changes or corrections in copy made by the author may be billed, as opposed to corrections necessitated by the printer's error for which there is no charge.

black the most common color of printing ink, popular for its high contrast value with both white and colored paper stocks; one of the four process colors.

black and white a monochromatic photograph displaying shades of black and gray. In art, an illustration created by applying a black medium to a white art board. In printing, reproductions of photos or art with black ink on white paper.

bleed a photograph that extends to the edge of a page on one or more sides, leaving no external margin.

bold face thicker, heavier type used for emphasis with lighter type face.

border an ornamental strip or design around a page, a photograph or artwork.

brightness in photography, light reflected by the copy; in paper, the reflectance or brilliance of the paper.

budget an estimate of income and expenses which serves as a financial plan for the magazine.

byline line at beginning or end of prose or poetry giving name of person who wrote it.

camera ready a finalized condition of artwork submitted by the staff so that it does not need retouching or finalizing by the printer's artists before being sent to the camera department; in printing—copy, especially art, that is finalized and ready to be sent to the camera department. (The camera department shoots a negative, from which offset printing plates are later made). Since camera ready artwork was not pasted up by the printer, it should cost considerably less than if the same artwork had been completely pasted up by the printer.

candid an unposed photograph which shows action.

capital letters (caps) upper case letters used to begin sentences and proper nouns.

caption a short piece of copy that describes the persons, action or scene of a photograph or illustration; answers obvious reader's questions. Captions are essential for feature photographs. Once known as a *cutline*.

center of interest the focal point of a picture, page or spread.

character a letter, numeral, punctuation mark or other part of the alphabet.

character count the number of characters, including spaces between words, that make up a piece of copy, caption, title or headline.

clip art artwork cut from one source and also used in the design of a printed material, such as advertising logos, mascots or symbols. Well executed student artwork is always preferable to clip art. Also known as *canned art*.

close register the printing of two or more colors within 6 points of each other, either partially or completely overlapped, resulting in increased printing precision to assure proper alignment of the colors.

coated paper paper which has a surface coating, giving it a smooth finish. If the magazine can afford it, coated paper can greatly enhance high quality artwork and photography.

collage a work of art that is composed by pasting on a single art board various materials such as photos. Feature magazines should always avoid collages; literary-art publications can usually find better ways to display artwork.

collate the gathering of sheets of signatures in correct sequence.

colophon an inscription, usually at the end of the magazine, giving certain publishing credits or technical printing information.

color the hue, saturation and brightness of an object or substance.

color in lieu of black use of a colored ink, rather than black ink, to print all page elements in a flat or series of flats. Consult your printer to determine what, if any, additional charges may apply here.

color printing usually refers to the reproduction of a full-color photograph or art illustration with the four process colors of yellow, magenta, cyan and black; also refers to the use of ink other than black.

color separation the process of filtering each of the four process colors from a full-color photograph or artwork and recording each color on separate pieces of film.

complicated layout a layout design that incorporates thin tool lines, rounded corners, large areas of tinted background, trapped halftones and/or several instances of close register making the spread difficult to produce.

composition in photography, the relativ[e] position of one subject to another in a pho[to]tograph and the relative postition of a sub[-]ject to the edge of the photograph; in typog[-]raphy, the arrangement of type to fit [a] specified copy area of the layout.

computerized composition type input o[n] a keyboard and subsequently run through [a] computer which makes line-end, hyphena[-]tion and other typographic decisions[.] Sometimes, a computer-produced diskett[e] or "floppy" is then used as input for pho[-]totypesetting equipment.

condensed type a narrow type face.

contact print a photographic print made b[y] placing a film negative directly on prin[t] paper and exposing to light, used to proo[f] several negatives on one sheet of prin[t] paper.

continuous tone a black and white photo[-]graph or artwork that has a continuou[s] range of tones from dark to light.

contrast the degree of tonal gradation[s] between dark and light areas in an origina[l] or reproduction.

copy to a journalist or nonfiction writer, th[e] words written to tell a story or describe a[n] event; to a printer, all written materials, art[-]work and photos to be printed.

copy block the layout space allocated fo[r] the written text, as distinguished from th[e] space allocated for captions, titles or head[-]lines, photographs or art.

copyfitting determining the amount o[f] manuscript copy that can fit into a give[n] area for a specified size and style of type[.]

copyright the exclusive right for the creato[r] or owner of original literary, artistic or pho[-]tographic material to make, distribute an[d] control copies of that work for a specifie[d] number of years, as guaranteed by law[.] Copyright registration materials are avail[-]able by writing the Register of Copyright[,] Library of Congress, Washington, D.C.

cropping marking a photograph to indicat[e] the image area to be reproduced, usuall[y] done to eliminate unnecessary areas withi[n] the photograph and improve compositio[n] thereby increasing the impact of the princi[-]ple subjects in the photograph.

crop marks marks on the white margin o[f] photographic prints or masking tape over

22—Magazine Fundamentals

lays on transparencies. See *cropping*.

cross gutter bleed a photograph or art that extends across the middle of the spread from the left-hand page to the right-hand page. See *bleed, spread*.

cyan in printing, one of the four process colors consisting of equal parts of blue and green; in photography, one of the three subtractive primary colors. See *subtractive color*.

deboss the reverse of the embossing process; letters or artwork are pressed down into the surface of a page or cover.

density a measure of the relative blackness of photographic images.

depth of field in photography, area of acceptably sharp focus, beyond and in front of the actual point of focus.

descender the lower stroke to those lower case letters that extend below the base line, for example, g, p.

die an engraved metal plate for cutting or embossing an image on paper or a cover.

die cut a pattern or design that is cut out by a die and removed from a page or cover so that part of the next page is visible.

direct line a special effect that eliminates the gray areas from a continuous tone original.

dot the individual element of a halftone.

double-page spread Sometimes abbreviated D.P.S. See *spread*.

dropout lack of dots in a light area of a halftone reproduction.

dropout halftone artificial lightening of continuous tone art to produce pure white in the light gray areas.

dropout mask an overlay on a piece of artwork or a photograph on which part of the art or photo is isolated and designed for special reproduction camera treatment.

dummy a mock-up of spreads or sections of the magazine to show the size, shape, form, sequence and general style for the purpose of content planning. If the printer is doing your pasteup, he or she will usually require a mini-dummy from you to guide the person doing pasteup.

duotone a black and white continuous tone original that is reproduced in two colors with two halftone negatives; one color is usually black. This special effect usually incurs additional printing costs; if well done with a creative or mood photograph, it can sometimes make a good photograph into a great special effect. More often than not, it is poorly done and yields disastrous results, such as a poor choice of the one or both of the colored inks, resulting, for example, in purple people.

elite the smaller of the two most common typewriter faces, having 12 characters to a linear inch. See *pica*.

emboss to produce a raised design on a cover or paper with a die.

emphasis face bold or italic type used in conjunction with a matching regular type face to stress important words or sentences.

enamel a term applied to a coated paper or to a coating material on a paper.

enlargement an increase in the size of a photo or artwork.

external margin the white space on the outside of a spread. See *internal spacing*.

eye flow in layout, the natural eye movement from left to right as English is read. The best layouts are designed with pleasing eye flow.

fake duotone a halftone printed over a screened block of color to give the effect of a duotone.

family one particular design or style of type in all its sizes, weights, widths and variants. See *font, type, type face, text type*.

film a thin plastic-like flexible material coated with a light-sensitive emulsion used for taking photographs.

final art art that is submitted ready for printing without having to be retouched, cleaned, or finalized by a company artist.

flat in photography, having very little variation in brightness between light and dark areas; low contrast.

flop printing a photograph from the wrong side of the negative, creating a reversed or mirror image.

flush left copy that is set so the left margin forms a perfect vertical line. This is the most easily read format. See *flush right, justified*.

flush right copy that is set so that the right margin forms a perfect vertical line. This is less easily read than *flush left* and should only be used for special designs. See *flush left, justified*.

foil stamp the application of thin, colorful metallic foil to a cover or end sheet using a die with heat and pressure.

folio a page number, best located at the bottom of each page. See *folio tab*.

folio tab a short piece of copy adjacent to the *folio* which identifies the section, chapter or text appearing on that page. Most often found in feature magazines, but sometimes used effectively in literary-art magazines. See *folio*.

font the complete set of all letters, numerals, ligatures and punctuation marks of a type face. See *family, type face*.

form the pages printed on one side of a sheet of paper.

format the size, style, shape, printing requirements, etc. of any magazine, book or printed piece.

four-color the printing of a color photograph using the four process colors. See *full-color, spot color*.

F-stops the settings that indicate the size of the opening or aperture in the lens of a camera.

full-color a color photograph or the four color reproduction of a color photograph. See *four-color, spot color*.

full-scale in photography, having a broad range of tones from vivid whites through numerous gray tones to rich, saturated blacks.

galley type that has been set on film-like paper by a modern photocompositor in preparation for proofreading and printing; originally referred to a tray that held metal type.

gatefold a page, larger than the trim size of a book, folded one or more times so as not to extend beyond the edges of the book.

ghosting a special effect that overexposes a photograph or artwork so that it will be lightened and have less contrast when reproduced.

glossy a shiny photographic print that, because of its smooth surface and high contrast lustre, provides optimum reproduction quality.

grain in book binding, a fine textured pattern embossed on the entire surface of a cover; in photography, the clumping or overlapping of silver particles in the negative causing a speckled or mottled effect in a photograph.

graphic arts camera a special camera that photographs black-and-white or color originals through either a halftone screen or a special effects screen to produce halftone negatives, special effects negatives or color separations. Printers use this type of camera to prepare printing plates from camera-ready artwork. See *halftone, halftone negative, color separations, camera-ready artwork*.

graphics the art or representation of decoration and writing or printing on flat surfaces together with the techniques and crafts associated with each.

gutter the inner space between two pages of a spread where the paper runs into the spine. See *spread*.

halftone the printed reproduction of a black and white continuous tone original, the image being reproduced with a pattern of tiny dots that vary in size.

halftone dot the individual element of a halftone. Collectively, halftone dots represent the image of a continuous one original when it is printed on paper. The largest dots occur in the darkest areas of the original; gray areas are reproduced by smaller dots; and white areas are reproduced by the absence of dots. See *highlight*.

halftone negative a negative reproduction of a continuous tone original, made on film using a halftone screen.

halftone screen a plate of glass or plastic containing fine wires set in a crisscross pattern, usually 133 or 150 lines per inch, used in a graphics arts camera to transform continuous tone originals into a pattern of halftone dots. See *continuous tone original*.

headline the title for a story, written to highlight the most import angle of the article. Headlines contain a noun and active verb; titles do not usually have an expressed verb. Feature magazines should use headlines except for literary materials; literary/literary-art magazines usually use titles for fiction, poetry, art and photography. See *title*.

highlight the lightest or whitest parts in a picture, represented in a halftone by the finest dots or by the absence of all dots or lines. See *halftone dot*.

indent starting from the first line of a flush left paragraph a few spaces to the right. Used with an initial letter especially in lengthy prose pieces. See *flush left, initial letter*.

index a detailed listing of every piece (fiction, nonfiction, poetry, art, photography or the like) which appears in the magazine. Required in student yearbooks but not in magazines, which usually use a contents listing instead.

initial letter a large letter which is set at the beginning of a block of copy. Its base must align with one of the lines of following text. Initial letters can be either stick-up (into white space above first line of text) or set-in (to the first one, two or three lines of text).

internal spacing white space on a layout between page elements; this spacing should be consistent on a spread. See *external margin*.

italic the style of letters that slant forward, in distinction from upright, or Roman letters. Used for words requiring emphasis. See *bold face, emphasis type*.

justified copy that is set so that both the left and right margins are flush, forming a straight-sided column.

keyboard the input mechanism which records onto paper or magnetic tape, disc or into an electronic memory.

kicker smaller-sized headline used above regular headline, especially in feature magazines.

layout the arrangement of body copy, headlines, captions, photographs, art and white space for a spread.

layout forms gridded sheets of paper either proportionate to or the exact dimensions of a magazine's trim size, used for planning and illustrating the layout arrangement of each spread. Graph paper with 1 pica square grid layout can be used as an inexpensive substitute for printer's layout forms.

layout style a general layout format to be followed throughout a book to provide visual unity.

leaders in typography, repetition of dots separating columns of material (usually found on contents pages).

leading (pronounced "ledding") the space between lines of type. Also called linespacing.

line art an illustration in which all drawn marks are black with no gradations of gray; line copy.

line negative a film negative reproduction of line copy.

lithography the process of producing an image on a specially treated metal plate with a greasy or oily substance and of making an inked impression on paper by direct contact with the metal plate, as opposed to using an intermediate rubber blanketed cylinder as with offset lithography. See *offset lithography*.

loose register the printing of two or more inks on a page so that the different colors are printed at least one-half pica (6 points) from each other. See *close register*.

lower case the small letters of a type face.

magenta in printing, one of the four process colors, consisting of equal parts of blue and red; in photography, one of the three subtractive primary colors. See *subtractive color*.

margin the white space between page elements and the edge of the page. See *external margin, internal spacing*.

markup the indication of desired type size and spacing as marked up beside the copy.

mask See *dropout mask*.

matte finish a photographic or printing paper, characterized by a dull, smooth surface. See *coated paper*.

measure width or depth of type matter, usually in picas. See *pica*.

mezzotint a special effect that reproduces a continuous tone original with a roughened, specular appearance. Usually costs extra at the printer's. See *continuous tone original*.

moire in printing, the undesirable screen pattern caused by incorrect screen angles; often the result of submitting photographs cut from printed material instead of original photographic prints.

montage printing two or more negatives on one piece of paper, or cutting and mounting two or more photos or drawings to make one illustration.

mortice a window or clear space in a photograph or artwork that is photo-mechanically dropped out so that a typographical message may be inserted; not usually the best way to combine type and photographs.

natural spread the two center pages of a signature, so named because they are the only two pages in a signature that are printed side by side. This spread is perfect for cross-the-gutter graphics, photographs or text, since there are no alignment problems. See *signature, spread*.

negative a photographic image that reverses the tones of the original image. On a negative, the dark areas of the original image are represented by light areas and vice versa.

negative stripping a printing operation in which halftone and special effects negatives and color separations are taped in position on a line negative.

odd shape photos any photograph having sides other than right angles, such as circles, triangles, trapezoids, octagons, etc.; usually a poor design substitute for the standard rectangular photograph.

Glossary—23

offset lithography a printing process in which a metal plate is used to make an inked impression on a rubber blanketed cylinder which transfers the impressions to the paper being printed, as opposed to making the impression directly from the plate to the paper as with lithography. Most student magazines are printed using offset lithography. See *lithography*.

offset press a printing press with rubber blanketed cylinders, used in offset lithography.

one color printing printing a job with only one color, usually black; the most common and inexpensive means of printing.

opacity the physical property of quality paper which does not allow printed impressions on one side of the paper to show through to the other side. Sometimes called bleedthrough.

options printing extras not specified in the basic bid price from the printer. Late inclusions of options usually results in higher than expected printing costs.

original artwork or photograph submitted by the staff to the printer from which halftone or special effects negatives or color separations are made and printed impressions are reproduced. See *halftone, special effects negatives, color separations*.

overlay a method of preparing complicated black and white or multicolor artwork in which each of the parts to be printed in each color (or large tint areas, shadow letters, etc.) are prepared on a transparent acetate or paper sheet which is permanently attached and registered to an art board. Also used for masking and marking special instructions on one color artwork. Or, with no special instructions, as a protective flap. See *art board, artwork, register, register marks*.

overprint the printing of one color over another color or the same color such as printing black type over a black and white halftone. Also called overburn. Select its use with care: it may be hard to read.

page one side of a leaf of a magazine or book; not a sheet which has two sides.

page elements the photos, art, copy block, captions, headlines/titles and white space that make up the layout design of a page or spread. See *external margins, internal spacing*.

page proof a proof of an individual page.

paste-up the process of actually pasting type, line art and blocks representing halftones on a special layout form (or art board) from which a line negative is shot; also, the special layout form with pasted-up type, line art and photo blocks.

photocomposition the technique of setting type photographically. Also called phototypesetting or "cold type" composition.

photogram an image produced without a camera by placing some object(s) directly onto photographic film or paper and then exposing to light.

photographic print a positive photograph produced on photographic paper by the transmission of light through a negative.

photomechanical techniques special effects created photographically by the printer with a graphic arts camera. See *graphic arts camera*.

photo silhouette a direct line special effect. See *direct line*.

pica a unit of measurement equal to 12 points or 1/6 inch; the larger one of the two most common typewriter faces, having 10 characters to a linear inch. See *elite, point, type*.

point a unit of measurement equal to 1/72 inch or 1/12 pica; a unit of paper, card and binder's board measurement equal to .001 inch. See *pica, point size*.

point size the measurement of a type face from the top of the highest ascender to the bottom of the lowest descender. See *ascender, descender, point, type face*.

positive a photographic image which corresponds to the original copy; the reverse of a negative. See *negative*.

posterization a special effect adapted from a direct line, in which, along with pure black and white values, a shade of dark gray is photomechanically reinserted. See *direct line, special effect*.

pre-separated art artwork created for multicolor reproduction by the artist on overlays with one color designated to each overlay, thus eliminating the need for photomechanical color separations prior to printing. See *artwork, overlay*.

press a machine for printing.

press run the running of a printing press for a specific job, signature, flat or color application.

print to produce inked images on paper or other surfaces either with direct pressure or by offsetting on an intermediate cylinder. See *lithography, offset lithography*.

process color the printing of yellow, magenta, cyan and black in various intensities, values and screens to reproduce full-color photographs or art. See *color, color printing*.

proportion the comparative relation between the width and height of photographs, artwork and copy, helpful in determining enlargement or reduction percentages and layout fit. See *enlargement, layout*.

register the correct relation or exact superimposition of two or more colored inks. See *close register, loose register*.

register marks small marks printed near the edge of the paper to aid in registering two or more colors while printing, then trimmed off so as not to appear in the book; in art, marks, usually small crossed inside circles, used on art overlays to show the exact position of the overlay in relation to the art board. See *art board, artwork, overlay, register*.

reverse reproduction of an image by printing around its basic shape but not inside; type is sometimes reversed out of a background area.

rub-on art commercially-prepared art aids that can be made into camera-ready art by rubbing the design or typographical character until it transfers from the acetate to the art board. See *art board, camera-ready art*.

rule line a black or colored line which is used to accent copy or photographs or other elements on a page. Best sizes are hairline, 1 point, 2 point.

saddle stitched a method of binding small, paper-cover books and magazines (96 pages or less) by stitching with wire staples or thread through the center fold. Most student magazines are saddle stitched.

sans serif a type style distinguished by characters that have no short finishing strokes at the ends of the main strokes, such as Helvetica, Univers and Franklin Gothic. See *serif, type*.

scale plan for proportionate reduction or enlargement of a photo or art to fit a given space. See *enlargement, layout*.

score to impress or indent a mark with a string or rule in the paper to make folding easier.

screen in a graphic arts camera, a plate glass or film with cross-ruled opaque lines used to break continuous tone illustrations, photographs and artwork into halftones; in stripping, film with uniform dot pattern used to create printed areas of a certain percentage density, such as 30%, 50% or 70%. See *continuous tone, graphic arts camera, halftone, halftone screen, stripping*.

screening/screen percentage printing a color or black in a lighter shade than its maximum density (which is defined as "100% solid color"). In full color reproductions, process color inks are usually screened to match the color density of the original. See *full-color, density process color*.

separation a negative of one or more images of a process color set, especially one taken through a color filter. See *pre-separated art, process color*.

serif a small finishing stroke at the end of the main stroke of a letter; a style of type, distinguished by characters having serifs, such as Palatino, Times Roman, Goudy and Century. See *sans serif, type*.

shutter a mechanical device in a camera that opens and closes for a measured length of time to allow photographic film or plates to be exposed to light.

signature all the pages printed on a sheet of paper. See *leaf, page*.

silkscreen a technique for applying opaque lacquer to a book cover by forcing the lacquer through desired areas of a fine mesh screen, made of silk, with a squeegee.

special effect any of a number of techniques that render a photograph as a mezzotint, etching, sunburst, etc. giving it visual appeal. One of the most common reasons for extra expense in printing, special effects are good examples of "less is more." See *mezzotint*.

special effect negative a negative reproduction of a continuous tone original, made on film using a special effect screen.

special effect screen in printing, a plate of glass or plastic containing fine wires set in any one of several special effect patterns, used in a graphic arts camera to distort the original to a special effect. In photography, any of several patterns on thin, clear acetate which can be used in a darkroom to create special effects in photographic prints.

specifications a description of the dimensions, materials, etc. needed for the production of a printed piece such as a magazine. Accurate specifications tell the printer precisely what you want him or her to print; in turn, the printer can tell you approximately what it will cost and how long it will take. Better specifications yield better control and pricing of the printing process—for you and the printer.

spot color the use of colored ink in printing other than for full-color reproductions. See *full-color, process color*.

spread two facing pages in a publication; used synonymously with double-page spread. Since the eye sees each spread as a single visual unit, spreads should be designed as one visual unit, instead of as two single pages which happen to be printed side-by-side.

stripping the positioning and fastening of halftone and special effect negatives and color separations on a layout line negative by use of small pieces of tape or liquid adhesive. See *halftone negatives, special effect negatives, separations, layout line negative*.

subhead a minor headline or title, usually set in a point size smaller than main headlines and titles but larger than body copy. Especially useful in long prose pieces such as essays and feature stories, subhead break up lengthy masses of type.

subtractive color a way of producing col by using the three subtractive primary c ors: cyan, magenta and yellow. Each sul tractive primary color absorbs (subtracts) complementary color from white light, lea ing behind the desired color.

sunburst a special effect that accentuat part of a photograph or artwork with radia ing lines. As with all special effects, "less more."

text type type used for text, usually 10 or 1 point, sometimes 8 point.

theme a central idea or concept, usual expressed as copy or an art illustratio repeated throughout the magazine, that un fies the message of the publication.

tint background a solid or screened area ink used as a background for halftone ph tographs, artwork or copy. It is not recon mended for covering an entire page spread.

tip-in an insert, usually of a different pap stock than the rest of the book, glued to bound page of the book.

title page a page at the beginning of th magazine that contains the magazine's tit year of publication, school or college nan as publisher, and the location (address, c state and ZIP code) of the school or colleg

tool line an area that separates a photograp or a design element from a solid or ti background; in the printed magazine, ma take on the color of the paper stock use

transparency a type of color film having positive image that is transparent to lig and suitable for projection; a slide.

trapped white space an area of whit space more than 2 picas by 2 picas separa ing two or more photographs or copy block and giving the appearance of disunity to th layout design.

trim edges three sides of a book or mag zine that are trimmed before casing it in cover.

trim size the final trimmed dimensions of book or magazine. Magazines usually use trim size of 8½" x 11".

type printed character(s).

type face a full range of characters, inclu ing letters, numerals and mark of punctua tion, in all point sizes.

typography the arrangement, style an design of letters, numerals and mark punctuation.

unjustified type which is set with on straight margin (usually the left) and on ragged margin (usually the right). See *flus left, flush right, justified*.

upper case the capital letters of a type fac See *lower case, type face*.

vignette a halftone with a background grad ually fading away and blending into the su face of the paper.

white space part of a layout design that not occupied by photograph, artwork, cop or tint background; so named because it the part of the page where the white paper visible. See *trapped white space*.

widow a short last line of a paragraph, les than half filled with type.

x-height the height of the letter x; the heigh of the main body of any lower case lette excluding ascenders or descenders. Typ faces of the same point size do not neces sarily have the same x-height. See *ascende descender, letter, type face*.

yellow one of the four process colors, con sisting of equal parts of red and green; i photography, one of the three subtractiv primary colors. See *four-color, proces color, subtractive color*.

24—Magazine Fundamentals